STAR TALES

NORTH AMERICAN INDIAN STORIES

Star Tales

Retold and Illustrated by
Gretchen Will Mayo

WALKER AND COMPANY
NEW YORK

Published simultaneously in Canada by
Thomas Allen & Son Canada, Limited, Markham, Ontario.

Book design by Laurie McBarnette

Library of Congress Cataloging-in-Publication Data

Mayo, Gretchen Will.
Star tales : North American Indian stories / by Gretchen Will
Mayo. — 1st pbk. ed.
p.   cm.
Includes bibliographical references.
Summary: A collection of Indian legends about the stars, moon, and
nighttime sky.
ISBN 0-8027-7345-1 (pbk.)
1. Indians of North America—Legends. 2. Stars—Folklore.
3. Moon—Folklore. [1. Indians of North America—Legends.
2. Stars—Folklore. 3. Moon—Folklore.] I. Title.
[E98.F6M35   1990]
398.26—dc20
[398.2]
[E]   90-12787
CIP
AC

Printed in the United States of America

Originally published in hardcover in 1987 by the Walker Publishing Company, Inc.

2   4   6   8   10   9   8   7   5   3   1

For Tom,
Meg, Molly and Ann

My appreciation and thanks
to Dr. Alice B. Kehoe
and
the Milwaukee Public Museum

CONTENTS

INTRODUCTION

Leaning close to a glowing campfire, a gathering of young people watch The Old One as he acts out a story. His wrinkled hands stroke the night air. He is describing Crane Woman's escape from her earthly husband, the greedy and evil Wolf Man. Crane Woman and her two starving sons have nowhere else to run from the wicked Wolf Man, but they find safety in the sky where they will become stars.

The young people are Native American Indians. The stories might have been told last night or a hundred years ago, for the tale of Crane Woman is an ancient one. Native American Indians have spun tales for one another for century upon century. Their stories reflect their ways of life, their beliefs, and the laws of their tribes.

Some of the storytellers were farmers. They told tales of Corn Maiden. Other Indians roamed the plains, hunting buffalo. From their tribes came stories of ghostly buffalo herds. There were whalers and salmon fishermen, trappers and shepherds, basket weavers and potters. The countless ancient Indian tribes were as different as the land was different across the continent, but they all shared a love for storytelling.

Native American ancestors were keenly aware of the land and the sky that surrounded them. They felt that all creation was connected. They believed that spirits could appear in all things, from rocks to ravens to falling stars. When they looked at the night sky, they joined all the world's people in imagining what the stars could be. They wove many tales about the sky country.

The gifted Indian tale-spinners have passed along the thread of their Native American stories from generation to generation. Sometimes they have reverently conformed to the original myths. Often they embellished the tales with details springing from their own imaginations. The stories in this collection are another link in that creative storytelling tradition and are offered with a sense of appreciation for what has been told before.

STAR TALES

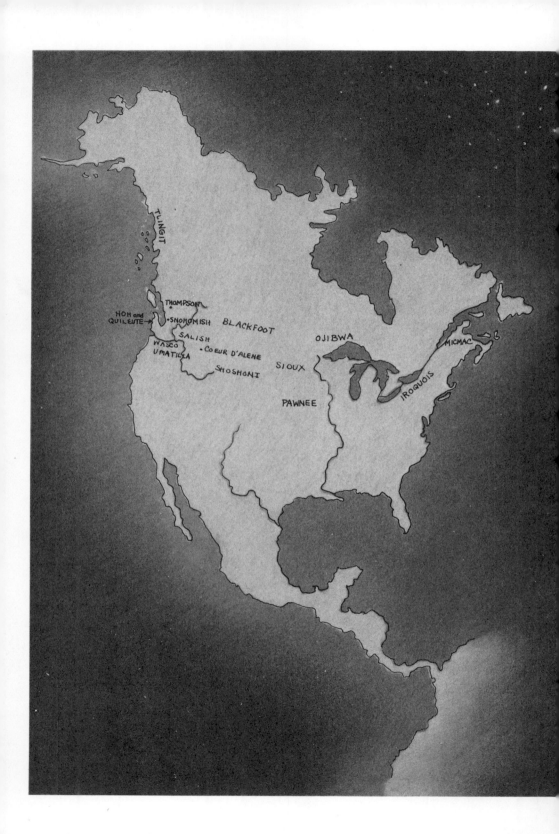

Coyote Makes the Constellations

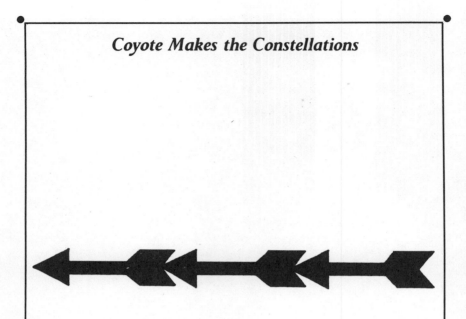

Some Native American ancestors looked at the night sky and saw the outlines of familiar animals dotted by stars. Other Indians, though, imagined that each individual star was a person, animal, or object in the sky country.

The Wasco Indians told a tale to explain how these star "pictures" appeared in the sky. The Wascos were part of the Chinook tribe which lived on the southern shores of the Columbia River in Oregon.

Coyote is a trickster and one of their legendary heroes. Although he is an animal, Coyote talks and behaves like a human. His many tricks confuse and frustrate the people but, when it is convenient, he also gives them gifts. He has powers greater than any human, and he likes to be admired. Even though Coyote is not to be trusted, the Indians often benefit from his antics in their tales.

COYOTE MAKES THE CONSTELLATIONS

One night, Coyote was making his way through the fields when he came upon five wolf brothers. They were seated with their dog, looking at the sky.

"Why do you sit and look above?" asked Coyote.

"It's no business of yours," answered one of the wolves.

"Such unpleasant fellows," thought Coyote to himself. He sat down beside them anyway. The wolf brothers paid no attention, but continued to gaze at the sky.

"What is it you see up there?" inquired Coyote after a time.

"Nothing!" snapped the wolf brothers. Still they stared at the stars. Long minutes passed. No one made a move.

"Well, I see you have truly lost your wits," muttered Coyote, and he got up to leave.

"If you must know," growled the oldest wolf, "we see a bear up there, and we are watching it." Coyote sat down and looked again. Sure enough, he saw among the stars the outline of a large bear.

Finally, Coyote said, "Let's all go up and take a close look at that bear."

3

"How can we do that?" scowled the wolves.

"First I will shoot that small star with my bow and arrows," boasted Coyote. The others laughed as he shot his first arrow, but they could not see it come down again. Coyote shot another arrow, and then another. Now the laughing stopped. All the star-watchers saw a chain of arrows hanging from the sky. Coyote continued to shoot his arrows, and soon the chain reached the place where they were sitting.

"Now we can go see that bear!" exclaimed Coyote. "Follow me!" And he began climbing up the arrow chain.

When all the animals had reached the sky, Coyote cautioned, "Don't get too close to the grizzly bear. You might make it angry." So each of the brothers and their dog found a place in the sky where they sat quietly and looked at the bear. The bear looked back.

Coyote looked around at the others sitting there in the sky, and he sighed. "They make such a nice picture. I'd like to keep them this way always," he said to himself. Then he thought, "If I keep the sky as it is, people below will look up and say, 'Coyote made that beautiful picture for us!'" So Coyote scampered quickly down the arrow chain, removing each of the arrows as he went.

When Coyote reached earth again, he took his arrows and disappeared over the hill. The wolf brothers and their dog still sit in the sky quietly watching the grizzly bear while the bear looks back.

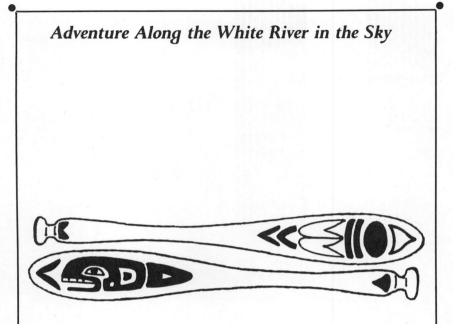

Today the great stroke of stars across the night sky is called the Milky Way. There once must have been almost as many different stories about the Milky Way as there were Indian tribes in North America. Some tribes believed it was the path that birds took in their migrations. The Pawnees said it was the pathway taken by spirits of the dead to the Southern Star, where they would live for eternity. The Snohomish of Puget Sound were whalers and fishermen who saw the Milky Way as a river and the scene of a conflict between the people of earth and sky.

ADVENTURE ALONG THE WHITE RIVER IN THE SKY

The Milky Way

When all the world was cold and dark, there was once a man who made canoes so tight and strong they rode the water like sleek silver fish. The canoemaker loved his work so much that he would begin every day at dawn, before the stars had left the sky, and would work late into the night. He hammered and pounded, scraped and rubbed, until his fine vessels stood worthy of the most angry waters.

Above him, in the heavens, the great chief of the sky people raged at the endless hammering. Finally, to restore silence, he sent down four of his men to capture Canoemaker.

Now across the vast land, this man alone could make such fine canoes. When the people of his village found out that he was gone, they searched everywhere for him. They looked across the frozen hills, along the streams, and even under the unfinished canoes. Finally, at the far end of the village, they found an old man who whiled away his sleepless hours looking out his window. He told them of the canoeman's capture.

The villagers wrung their hands and pulled at their hair. "What will we do without our canoemaker?" they wailed.

Amid the complaining and the crying, the old man raised his voice. "When I was a boy, storytellers said the sky could be reached by making a chain of arrows," he recalled.

The people, ready to try any means, took up their bows and set about shooting a flurry of arrows into the air. Like a cloud of mosquitoes, the arrows flew against the heavens. But not one rose high enough to stick in the sky. Robin, who had been flitting about from tree to tree, finally came forward to help them. He flew up and thrust the first arrow into the sky, then Canoemaker's people added theirs until a chain of arrows hung all the way down to the village.

Then the villagers began to climb into the heavens. They were very quiet so the great chief of the sky people would not hear them coming.

When the last of the villagers had made his way through the hole in the sky, Robin began at once to snoop around the sky country. First he found the

village of the sky people along the Great White River in the Sky. Then he found the canoemaker tied to the roof of a house. After assuring the canoemaker that help was coming, Robin raced back to alert the people.

By now Robin was getting cold, but he wanted to snoop around some more. While he was shivering about the sky country, poking here, nosing there, Robin began to feel something warm and went to investigate. Along the Great White River he came upon a group of sky people gathered around a fire. Robin had no idea what this strange glowing thing was, for the lower world had never been given fire. But how he loved the warmth! "Whatever this is, we should have some of it in our village," Robin said to himself.

Cautiously, he tried to move close to the fire to take some back to earth. Each time he came near, the sky people circling the fire pushed him back into the cold. Robin was angry. He found Beaver, and they made a plan.

Beaver floated down the Great White River to the

place where the sky people were gathered around the fire. As he had expected, some of the children saw Beaver and began to chase and tease him. Beaver played their game, but managed to creep closer and closer to the fire.

Just as Beaver was able to draw up to the fire, the people from Canoemaker's village came into camp to rescue their friend. The sky people jumped with a roar and charged after them.

Beaver saw his chance and wasted no time. In the confusion, he skittered up to the fire, snatched a flaming stick, and ran off to the hole in the sky.

Meanwhile, Robin led Canoemaker's people to the rooftop where they untied their friend. They all ran along the shore of the Great White River until they reached the hole in the sky.

The chief of the sky people came thundering after them, but Canoemaker and his people made their way out of the sky and down the arrow chain safely.

Afterward, as all the village people warmed themselves around Beaver's fire, the canoemaker thanked the villagers. "I will never make the great chief of the sky people angry again," he promised. That is why Canoemaker and his people never build their canoes early in the morning or late at night.

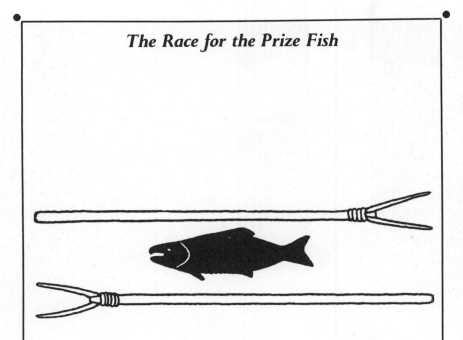

Some of the brightest stars in the sky sparkle in the constellation that we call Orion. The Inuit of Labrador said Betelgeuse, the largest of these stars, was a bear. The three stars of Orion's belt were said to be three hunters, and the row of stars hanging below the belt was the hunter's sled.

The Indians of our Southeast said Betelgeuse was not a bear but a bee tree. The other stars were said to be three hunters who had an ax, a deerskin bag, and a ladle. They were hoping to find some honey.

The Umatilla Chinook of northeast Oregon saw something entirely different in the stars of Orion. Their star tale tells of two kinds of wind that blew through their country and a fish that was one of their favorite foods.

THE RACE FOR THE PRIZE FISH

Belt and Sword of Orion

Ever since the time that the stars were placed in the heavens, there has been a race going on among the sky people. Two canoes race, as they always have, toward a large salmon floating in a river of the sky. The three bright stars in one canoe are the Cold North Wind brothers. The three Chinook Wind brothers paddle the other canoe. They are smaller stars but they are stronger, so they are winning the race. The Cold North Wind brothers will never win because of what happened long ago to the old grandfather of Chinook Wind.

At one time, so long ago none are left who saw it, the grandfather of Chinook Wind was a fine fisherman. Although age had slowed his bones, his mind was quick and sure. So he outwitted the fish and always brought home a large catch. The old grandfather's salmon were the envy of many, but especially of Cold North Wind. He was a blustery fellow who would like to have claimed the biggest and best of the fish for himself. But Cold North Wind always came too late. Because he was fierce and accustomed to having his way, Cold North Wind began to snatch the salmon from the old man when he returned to his lodge.

Chinook Wind worried when his grandfather seemed to be doing so poorly. One day while the old man fished, Chinook Wind hid. He saw his grandfather catch many salmon. But as the old man carried his baskets to his lodge, he was stopped by Cold North Wind, who demanded the fish. Chinook Wind stepped from his hiding place.

"You can't take my grandfather's catch!" shouted Chinook Wind.

"Yes, I can, because I am stronger!" bellowed North Wind.

"There are many kinds of strength!" challenged Chinook, and the two began to wrestle.

Now Cold North Wind was of a fearsome size and powerful. He stormed and raged and threw himself about. Chinook Wind seemed little match for him. But Chinook Wind had been taught since childhood to find his own strength, and he was clever. He was also quick. Before long, Cold North Wind was huffing and puffing as Chinook slipped again and again from his grasp.

Chinook Wind won the wrestling match, and Cold North Wind lay spent at his feet. Because Chinook Wind took away some of his strength, Cold North Wind can never win the race for the prize salmon.

The Antelope Chase

The Shoshoni Indians lived along the streams in what is now Nevada, Idaho, and Utah. They constantly moved in small groups from place to place searching for food. When food was plentiful, they preserved antelope and buffalo meat for winter use. Often in the long and dreary days of winter, if the lodge held a good supply of meat, the Shoshoni passed the time singing or telling stories. They told of Giant Big Horn, the Great Brown Bear of the Mountains, of ghosts and war heroes. Someone once said, "Never were there more marvelous storytellers and never were there more willing listeners."

THE ANTELOPE CHASE

Three-Stars-in-a-Row

There were once two brothers who were hunters. These brothers spent most of their days roaming the land, hunting antelope. The wife of the older brother, who wished she could see more of the world, was always left behind to tend the camp and watch her child. The unhappy woman decided to play a trick.

One day, after the hunters had left, she put on a pair of antelope horns and wrapped herself in an antelope hide. Then she stole off to a wooded place where the brothers were hunting. When the two brothers saw the antelope horns moving among the branches, they rushed to the thicket. The antelope had disappeared. They saw only the wife, who had removed her disguise and was picking berries.

"Did you see an antelope grazing near here?" asked the brothers.

"Oh, yes! And it was a mighty one!" the wife exclaimed. "But you're too late. It ran off into the forest."

The hunters thought they saw the huge antelope the next day as they hunted the forest, and the next day as well. Each time it escaped them. Each night

they dragged home with long faces. At the evening campfire the younger brother found few cheerful words as he told to the child the tale of the elusive antelope. But the older brother poked silently at the glowing embers of the fire and kept his thoughts to himself.

The next morning, the older brother decided to take a different route as his younger brother followed the antelope. Creeping silently from behind, he saw his wife taking off her disguise, but he remained hidden while he thought of a plan.

That night, when they all had returned to the campfire and were eating their meal, the oldest hunter said to his wife, "Tomorrow we will stay in camp to make more arrows. Leave the child with us while you go out to gather berries."

The wife quickly agreed and began humming as she unrolled the sleeping mats.

In the morning, when the sun had barely topped the hill, the woman hurried off. As soon as she was out of sight, the men set to work. Finding two logs, they laid them on their sleeping mats and covered them with blankets. Then they took up the antelope hides and horns and went off into the woods. They stopped where the wife came to draw water each day. Here the husband, his child, and his brother each dressed themselves in an antelope disguise and sat down to wait.

In a while, the wife came down the path humming to herself. She bent down to dip her hand into the clear water and, as she reached, she stopped. Mirrored in the water were the images of three antelope. The startled woman pulled back her hand slowly so she would not alarm the animals. She crept away from the water and down the path. When she had put some distance between herself and the antelope, she broke her silence and dashed back to camp calling, "Husband! Husband! Three antelope are grazing near the stream!"

No one moved in the camp, so when the wife saw the blanket-covered logs, she thought the men were still sound asleep. "There is no time!" she whispered to herself. "I'll get those antelope myself and surprise everyone." Snatching a bow and arrows, she ran back down the path.

When she reached the stream again, the excited woman could see antelope horns among the branches of the thicket. But as she crept closer, they began to move away. She raised her bow and placed her arrow. Antelope horns moved, shaking the branches and rustling the leaves. Then they disappeared beyond the thicket.

Through brush and brambles and groves, the woman chased the three antelope with her ready arrows. Out of the forest and over the hill they ran.

Then the woman saw that each antelope lacked two legs.

Her excitement dropped like a falling rock. She stopped, but only for an instant. With a screech of anger, the wife bolted forward again and disappeared over the hill in pursuit, legs pounding, shouts flying.

On some clear nights, three stars in a row with a fourth following can be seen crossing the heavens. These, say the ancients, are the two brothers and the child, with the wife still chasing them. They ran so hard, it is told, that they ran right into the sky.

During its migrations, the beautiful white snow goose flies over Coeur d'Alene Lake in western Idaho. Some say this was the large bird the Coeur d'Alene Salishans told about in their tales long ago.

For many centuries, people all over the world have seen the outline of a wide-winged bird among the stars. It seems to follow the path of the Milky Way. Many people called this constellation The Swan.

THE SPIRIT OF THE SNOW GOOSE

The Swan

In the cool shadows of a forest long forgotten, there was a clear lake whose deep waters mirrored the clouds by day and the stars by night. It was the resting spot of many creatures of the air. The loon, the blue-winged teal, and the mallard all found their way here. They would float with the clouds across the dark surface. They found rest in the trees rimming the lake and food in the waters.

One evening, three hunters came along a path which wound its way to the lake. They crept softly over the carpet of pine needles. They made no sound as they climbed over rocks. Finally, as the sun was sinking in the West, the three parted the thick branches of the green firs and peered across the waters. There they saw a splendid snow goose floating in the last light of day.

One of the hunters reached for his arrow. His friends stilled his hand. "This noble bird should not be robbed of its life," they said. But the hunter protested. The snow goose would be a great prize to take back to the village.

As they argued, the snow goose lifted its body. It

spread its wings to take flight. The impatient hunter, fearing the great white bird would get away, raised his bow and shot the snow goose. Drawing out its wings to their full span, the beautiful bird dropped to the lake. Then, as the last rays of sunset faded into night, it vanished in the deep, dark waters.

The three hunters stood as though frozen while a strange sadness filled the silence of the forest. Over the lake every last ripple smoothed itself.

Then, as the stars came out and were reflected in the waters, the waiting hunters saw the outline of a great bird take shape. They knew it was the spirit of the snow goose rising to the heavens. It still flies across the night sky, spreading its great wings across the waters of peaceful lakes.

The Tale of the Hungry Skunk

The Salish had many lively sky tales. In one tale, they said it was Coyote who was given the task of carrying the Moon across the sky each night. But as he traveled, they said, Coyote shouted gossip about all the people he saw below. The people were angry and took Coyote's job away.

The imaginative Salish saw another sky story in the constellations of Auriga and Perseus. This one was about a skunk and some women who were cooking camas roots for dinner. The camas root was a form of lily that was excellent eating and plentiful in many places in the high plateau country of Oregon, Washington, and Idaho where the Salish lived.

THE TALE OF THE HUNGRY SKUNK

Auriga, Perseus

Once, when darkness was marching across the sky, the women of the sky country were hurrying about the heavens preparing the evening meal. The men, who were sky fishermen, would be returning home soon and would be hungry.

The women had built a large pit where roots had been placed on hot rocks to cook. The roots had begun to steam, sending their fragrance in sweet-smelling clouds about the heavens.

A skunk wandered from among the trees and caught the scent of the cooking roots. This skunk was a lazy fellow, and it had been a long time since he had found himself a meal. So with his nose twitching and his stomach complaining, Skunk ambled off to see if he could get an easy meal.

It wasn't long before his nose led him to the edge of the village where every woman busied herself with some task. Past the lodges wandered the skunk, past babies sleeping in their cradles. At last Skunk saw the great cooking pit where even now more tender roots were being placed among the hot rocks to steam.

Skunk's stomach growled. He straightened himself

and began to march right up to the oven's circle. "I'm going to take my share of this tasty meal right now!" he said to himself.

"Mother, what is that animal walking toward us?" asked one of the small children helping at the pit.

"Aiiieeeee!" screamed the woman, snatching her child and running away.

"Aiiieeeee!" screeched the other women when they saw what had startled her. At once the place was in an uproar. Skunk marched right on.

But some of the women stayed at the pit. "Come away! Skunk will make you smell like rotten turnips!" cried one of their friends from her doorway.

"No skunk is going to steal my dinner," called back one stubborn woman from the pit. "I don't care how I smell!"

"You're not going to ruin my hard work!" shouted another to Skunk, who had stopped and was thinking about what he might do next.

Running back from their lodges, some of the women joined the others at the pit. There they clustered to protect their meal, sending threatening looks in Skunk's direction.

Skunk was amazed. He had never encountered anyone stubborn enough to challenge him. He looked at the women standing like great rocks around the steaming pit. "Maybe if I am quiet, they will grow tired and forget me," he thought. So he stood very still and waited.

The stubborn women would never give up. They are clustered to this day around their cooking pit. And just a few paces away stands the outline of Skunk, waiting even now for a chance to snatch an easy meal.

The Giant Elk Skin

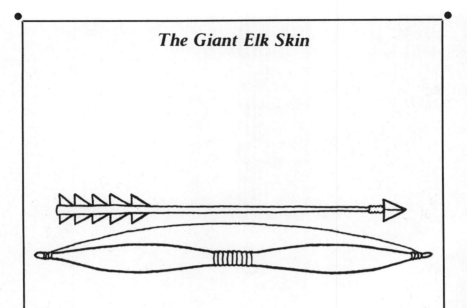

Cassiopeia's Chair looks like a giant W near the Milky Way. The Inuit saw this constellation as steps cut in the heavenly snows linking the sky country to earth. The Hoh and Quileute, who lived on the Olympic Peninsula of Washington, had a different idea. They were hunters and fishermen. Their tales tell about noble hunters whose arrows and hunting spears sometimes had spiritual powers and about super-animals of fearsome size and speed. These Northwest Coast Indians lived in a mild climate where food from both land and sea was plentiful, so their creativity spilled into all the arts. They wove elaborate blankets, built strong decorated wood houses, carved everyday tools into works of art, and spun tales of high adventure around their mythical heroes.

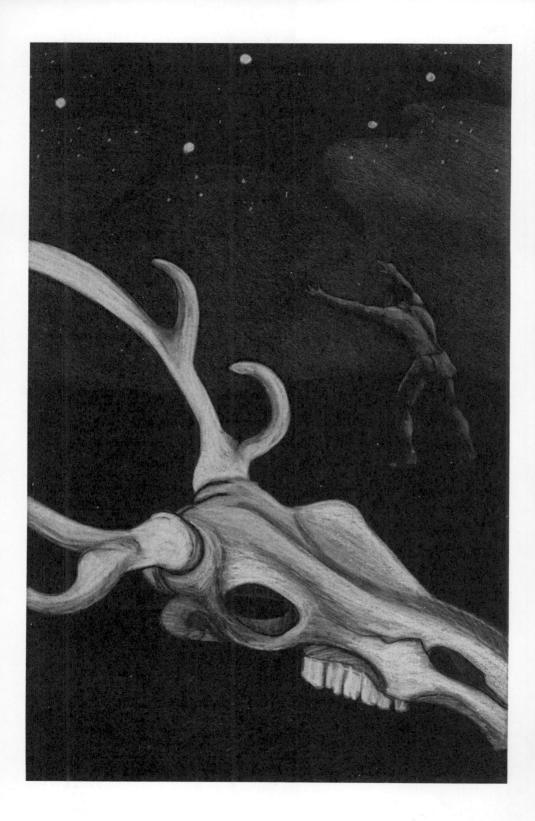

THE GIANT ELK SKIN

Cassiopeia

Long ago five brothers lived along a river. One day four of the brothers went out in their canoe to hunt and fish. When they came to a fork in the river, they pulled up and jumped out to see what hunting might bring them. They hadn't been hunting long when they met a lone man walking across the prairie. He asked what they were doing. When the brothers explained they were hunting for elk, the man said he knew where there was a large herd grazing. "If you will wait here," the man of the prairie said, "I will go ahead and chase the elk in your direction." The brothers all nodded their heads excitedly.

"But look," the man said, "my arrows are much better than yours. They have good medicine." Then he tricked them into trading their arrows for his, which in truth were worthless.

After the man of the prairie left, he changed himself into a giant elk. Then he thundered back to charge the brothers, killing all four of them. Their useless arrows had flown like straw in the wind against the hide of the huge animal.

When the four brothers failed to return, the fifth,

31

who was the youngest, set out to look for them. Reaching the fork in the river, he came upon their empty canoe and followed the footprints into the tall grass. Soon he too met up with the lone man of the prairie.

The man tried to trick the youngest brother as well, but the brother's guardian spirit was with him. He wasn't so easily fooled. "I trust the good medicine of my own arrows, for I made them with my own hands," he told the lone man.

When the brother refused to trade arrows, the man of the prairie walked on and out of sight. Soon the giant elk came charging after the fifth brother. With his own strong yew arrows, the brother shot the elk and it lay like a mountain on the prairie grass. "This mighty elk will feed many mouths," said the brother to himself. So he set to work preparing the elk meat to take home.

The youngest brother worked through the afternoon sun and into dusk. When he had finished, he began stretching the skin to dry it. "This great hide will have many uses," he thought. But as he struggled to stretch the huge skin, he found it was bigger than the whole prairie. He took the skin, gave a shout, and heaved the great skin into the sky. It is hanging there still. Stars shine, they say, in the holes where the youngest brother had driven stakes to stretch the skin.

As for the brother, he went home and, with his fine yew arrows, was never hungry.

The Birds of Summer

Some Native American legends say there was a time in which animals and humans lived, worked, and talked together. To the Ojibwas and other Algonkians, humans were one kind of "people" and animals were other kinds of "people." In an Ojibwa story about the Big Dipper, it is sometimes hard to guess which is which.

The Ojibwas tell us it is Fisher we see in the group of stars now called the Big Dipper. The Fisher is a lesser-known animal rather like a large mink. It is a cunning hunter and fierce fighter. The handle of the Big Dipper, the Ojibwas said, is Fisher's long, bushy tail.

THE BIRDS OF SUMMER

Big Dipper

It was the snow-swept time long ago when winter seemed never to end. All the people searched the land for some sign that the cold was melting, for summer's turn had arrived. But summer did not come.

As one day blew over the next, the anxious people wondered what to do and called a meeting. Huddled by the lodge fire, Fox, Muskrat, Beaver, and all the brothers of the tribe sat silently. They called upon the spirit of the animal whose name they had been given to help them find a solution. It was finally a cunning hunter named Fisher who spoke first. "Summer has not come because the birds of summer haven't returned," said Fisher, who had traveled many distant hills.

"What could have happened?" the people wondered. They talked about how the birds left each year as the trees turned golden.

"Never have the birds failed to return," said the most ancient of the elders.

While the people talked, Fisher was thinking. "I think I know who might be holding back the birds of summer," Fisher said shortly. "I have a selfish cousin

who wants all good things for himself. He has been named Cruel-Face. If he has captured the birds of summer, he will keep them."

With angry cries the people asked Fisher what they could do.

"This Cruel-Face has the will of a grizzly bear," Fisher answered. "But the bowl he fills for himself spills into the hands of his followers. To keep their comforts, his people jump to every command of this man-without-a-heart."

Fisher looked slowly around the campfire at the faces of Beaver, Caribou, Fox, and the others. "Prepare for a journey of ten sleeps," he said. "We must go to Cruel-Face to bring back the birds of summer."

The people agreed and parted to gather their things. In the morning Fisher lead his people out of camp and across the wind-swept fields.

They traveled through groves of barren trees. They walked along snow-blanketed game trails. They struggled through snow drifts and over frozen rivers. On the eighth day, cold still swept the ragged path. On every side, the world stretched grey and lifeless. Fisher told them to make camp for the night and to

look into the campfire for visions of a warm and sunny day. But some of the travelers mumbled about turning back.

The next morning, as they walked, the air began to feel warmer. The snow melted into the path and streams gurgled. By evening the travelers had removed their heavy robes. They came upon a wide, clear lake and laid down their packs in the sweet-smelling grass along the shore. It felt like spring.

When the people wondered at this change, Fisher pointed to the light of campfires across the lake. "That is the village of Cruel-Face. Warm breezes blow here because the birds of summer have never left this place," he said. "I will find Cruel-Face but you must help."

Then Fisher worked out a plan. Muskrat and Beaver were to start first before dawn. It was their job to make holes in the villagers' canoes and weaken their paddles. "When light begins to break," he said to Caribou, "you must swim into the lake. Fox will make barking noises to signal Caribou's crossing," he continued. "The rest of you must set up a commotion that all the world will hear." Fisher thought for a

37

moment, then he added, "There is one more thing. If the birds of summer come along, don't wait for me. Follow them!"

"We won't go without you," cried Caribou, "no matter what happens."

But Fisher silenced Caribou. "No, my friend, whatever happens, we must release the birds of summer. Their spirits cry out to travel their own path."

"We will see that nothing stops them!" Caribou said, and everyone agreed.

When dawn came, Fox's barking awakened Cruel-Face's people. Creeping from their lodges to see what the noise was about, they saw Caribou jumping into the lake. The eager villagers raced to their canoes with their bows and arrows. Caribou swam farther into the deep waters until only his shining antlers could be seen from the shore.

Fisher, hiding in the brush, watched the villagers hurrying off. Then he stole to the lodge of their chief.

He found Cruel-Face seated before a small fire in the center of his earthen floor. A collection of arrow shafts was at his side. All around him, filling the lodge from floor to ceiling, were stacks and stacks of birchbark boxes.

The bullish chief hunched toward the fire, using a long stick to jab again and again into a small heating pot resting on glowing logs. The pot held warm sturgeon glue which Cruel-Face was using to join feathers to arrow shafts.

Fisher saw that Cruel-Face was too busy making his arrows to notice him. Fisher peered through the smoky air and he listened. Then he crept toward the boxes.

Cruel-Face suddenly was on him like a snarling

wolf. But Fisher was quick. Snatching the glue stick from Cruel-Face's grasp, Fisher swished the dripping stick around, swabbing the mouth of the chief with a thick stroke of warm glue.

The astonished chief's hands shot to his face, where they stuck like a leech sticks to bare skin. He leaped up to cry out, but no cry came. His mouth was glued tight. Cruel-Face hopped around the lodge. Feathers flew. Boxes crashed. Sticks scattered.

The agile Fisher wasted no time. He dashed among the boxes, opening one, poking a hole in another. It was just as he had suspected. From the first box flew the thrushes and the warblers. From the second came finches and sparrows. Then came jays and wrens, swallows, woodpeckers, and bluebirds.

As his cousin thrashed about the lodge, Fisher opened every box. A rainbow cloud of birds rose from the lodge of the selfish chief. Like smoke it drifted out and over the lake where the people of Cruel-Face in their leaky canoes looked up.

"Look!" cried a warrior.

"Listen!" called others. "The birds of summer are getting away!" They began to whip their canoes around toward the village. Their paddles, damaged by Muskrat and Beaver, broke against the urgent strokes of the villagers. The canoes took on water and sank. Soon the people of Cruel-Face were swimming for shore.

As the birds of summer flew across the lake and over the forests, Fox, Caribou, Muskrat, Beaver, and all of Fisher's friends followed in great haste. Behind them a winter wind was already swirling around the lodges.

As for Fisher, he was still dodging the thrashings of

the angry chief, but one small box remained to be opened. Using an arrow shaft, Fisher poked a hole in the box and out darted a flurry of hummingbirds. They flashed and whirred around the head of Cruel-Face while Fisher dashed out of the lodge.

As a rabbit runs before the fox, Fisher ran from the chief to join his friends. He ran through the village, past the lodges, and smack into the raging mob of cold, wet villagers emerging from the lake.

Like an animal cornered, Fisher crouched, looking for an escape. Then he sprang for a tall tree. Climbing furiously, Fisher heard the panting of the angry villagers behind him. The tree shook. Branches snapped. Beyond him stretched only the sky.

"Brave Fisher!" whispered the stars. "Brave Fisher, you are our brother." Their voices called like the song of a hundred birds. Fisher thrust out his arms. Then, tearing from the grasp of the people, rising over treetops and hills, Fisher joined the friendly stars in the winter sky.

Beaver, Caribou, Fox, and the rest of the travelers returned to their village with the birds of summer. Before them, all the way, flowers bloomed and sleeping buds unfolded. But fear froze their hearts when the people thought about what might have happened to Fisher. After only one night, they set upon the path again to find their friend who had not returned.

The moon wasted from bright fullness to a thin sliver while Fisher's people searched for him. One night the people had gathered around the campfire when one small boy pointed to the sky. "I see Fisher there among the stars!" he said.

The people looked. Then they looked again. "Brave

Fisher has escaped to the sky country!" they mur-
mured excitedly one to the other. Then they hurried
to tell the story of Fisher and the birds of summer to
all the people of the village.

"We will keep those birds of summer for ourselves
from this day on," some of the villagers cried when
they heard the story. "We can make sure the warm
winds of summer always blow across our land."

But others looked up at the sky and asked, "What
would Fisher say about this?"

"Fisher would say the birds of summer should be
free to be themselves," said Fox, and many agreed.

That is why things are as they are. For half of the
year the people walk lightly in warm breezes. They
smell the fragrance of a thousand flowers and work to
the song of the meadowlark. But when the traveling
moon appears in the heavens, the birds of summer
take wing. Cold winds blow. The sun sinks lower in
the sky and snow sweeps the path. Then the people
search the winter sky for Fisher and make the long
nights pass more quickly sharing stories about their
brave friend and the birds of summer.

WHERE THE TALES BEGAN

1. ***COYOTE MAKES THE CONSTELLATIONS*** was collected in 1921 by Lucillus V. McWhorter.

2. ***ADVENTURE ALONG THE WHITE RIVER IN THE SKY:*** Dr. Herman Haeberlin heard this story from the Snohomish but died before he was able to publish it. Erna Gunther Spier wrote a version for him in 1924.

3. ***THE RACE FOR THE PRIZE FISH*** was also recorded by Lucillus V. McWhorter, who heard it from the Wascos.

4. ***THE ANTELOPE CHASE*** was told by Tom Austin to Robert H. Lowie who recorded it for the American Folklore Society.

5. ***THE SPIRIT OF THE SNOW GOOSE*** is based on a brief fragment found in the Memoirs of the American Folklore Society, 1917.

6. ***THE TALE OF THE HUNGRY SKUNK*** was crafted from comments written by Franz Boaz in 1917.

7. ***THE GIANT ELK SKIN*** is based on parts of a story recorded in 1909 by L.V.W. Walters.

8. ***THE BIRDS OF SUMMER*** is based on parts of a story recorded in 1919 by William Jones.

GLOSSARY

Alaskan panhandle—the southward extending Pacific coastline of the state of Alaska

Antelope—the mammal known in North America as the antelope is actually the pronghorn, and is the swiftest of all North American mammals

Arrow shaft—the long stem to which the head and feathers of an arrow are attached

Auriga—constellation also called "The Charioteer", located between Perseus and Gemini

Ax—handled tool with a sharpened end used for chopping

Beaver—a large rodent with a broad, flat tail. With its long front teeth, the beaver cuts trees which it uses to build dams and dens along streams.

Betelgeuse—a very bright star of the first magnitude seen near one shoulder of Orion, the constellation also called "The Hunter"

Big Dipper—the seven most obvious stars (which resemble a dipper) in the constellation Ursa Major or Big Bear.

Big Horn—a wild sheep. The males have large curling horns.

Birchbark boxes—lidded containers made by lacing together strips of bark from the birch tree

Boötes—also known as "The Herdsman." The handle of the Big Dipper points to this constellation.

Camas root—the edible bulb of the camas plant, a member of the lily family

Canoe—a long, narrow boat made of wood, bark or hides. Canoes made from birchbark were lightweight and easy for one or a few to carry. Some dugout canoes, made from huge logs, could carry more than fifty people. These were often decorated.

Caribou—a member of the deer family living in northern forests and bogs. Unlike other deer, both males and females have antlers.

Cassiopeia's Chair—a W-shaped constellation located between Andromeda and Cepheus

Chickadee—a small, lively bird with grey back and wings

Chinook wind—along the Pacific coast this is a warm wind which comes from the southwest. When it blows down the mountains in winter and early spring, it often melts snow at the base of the slopes.

Clearing—an area without trees

Constellation—a group of stars which appear to resemble a person or object

Corona Borealis—also known as the Northern Crown, a small constellation which seems to be a broken circle, between Hercules and Boötes

Council house—meeting place for the tribal council

Coyote—a swift, cunning mammal related to, but smaller than, the wolf. There are many American Indian tales about Coyote.

Eagle plume—a cluster of feathers worn as an ornament

Elk—the largest member of the deer family. Older males have large, many-tinted antlers.

Fir—an evergreen of the pine family

Fisher—a dark brown forest mammal related to weasels. Fishers are fierce hunters.

Fixed Star—also known as Polaris or The North Star

Fox—a sly, cunning mammal of the dog family having a bushy tail

Good medicine—helpful spiritual powers

Grazing—to feed on the vegetation

Great White River in the Sky—the name given by some Native Americans to the Milky Way

Grizzly Bear—a large and powerful bear of a brownish-yellow color

Guardian spirit—a supernatural being that was a personal spiritual helper and the source of a man's or a woman's power

High Plateau Country of Oregon—the Columbia plateau covering most of eastern Oregon. Much of this area is rugged and mountainous.

Horizon—the place where earth and sky seem to meet

Horned Owl—a large owl with tufts of feathers resembling horns on either side of its head

Labrador—a large peninsula in northeastern Canada bordered by Hudson Bay and the Atlantic Ocean

Ladle—a utensil used for dipping up liquid

Leech—a segmented worm which usually feeds on blood. Most live in water.

Migrations—the regular journey from one region to another for feeding and breeding

47

Milky Way—seen as a broad, irregular band of light stretching across the night sky, it is actually the light of billions of stars in our own galaxy

Morning Star—the last star visible in the sky after daybreak. The Morning Star is a planet, not a real star (usually the planet Venus.) Some ancients said Morning Star was a hunter among the sky people.

Mosquitoes—small insects with long legs. The female feeds on the blood of mammals.

Muskrat—mammal about the size of a small house cat which has dense dark brown fur and lives along streams and rivers. Water vegetation is its main food and the building material for its houses.

North Star—also known as *Polaris*. This is the star in the Northern Hemisphere toward which the axis of the earth points. As a result, when we look at the sky, all of the stars seem to circle around this star.

Northwest Coast—an area of the North American Pacific Coast extending northward from Northern California to Alaska

Nova Scotia—includes a peninsula of the Canadian mainland as well as Cape Breton Island and extends into the Atlantic Ocean northeast of Maine

Olympic Peninsula of Washington—a rugged mountain region in the northwest corner of Washington State bordered by the Strait of Juan de Fuca on the north and the Pacific Ocean on the west

Orion—a constellation that represents a hunter with a belt and sword. It is a winter constellation and has more bright stars than any other.

Perseus—a constellation located between Taurus ("The Bull") and Cassiopeia

Planet—one of the large heavenly bodies which revolve around our sun. At night planets reflect the light of our sun and look like stars, but are not. Ancient people noticed that the planets moved on their own individual paths across the heavens.

Pleiades—a bright cluster of stars in the constellation Taurus or "The Bull." Six or seven of the stars are visible to the average eye.

Polaris—another name for the North Star

Potlatch—at these lavish feasts, the host gave away valuable gifts to guests

Prairie—mostly level, grass-covered plains

Puget Sound—a huge bay between the Olympic Peninsula and the Cascade Mountains in Washington State. It is connected to the Pacific Ocean by the Strait of Juan de Fuca.

Robin—a migratory bird commonly known for its red breast

Salmon—a fish. The Pacific Salmon is known for the long journeys it makes upstream to its breeding grounds.

Saw-whet—a small owl with a harsh voice

Skunk—a cat-sized animal which sprays a foul smelling scent when threatened

Smoke hole—an opening constructed in houses, tipis, and lodges so that smoke from the fire could escape

Snow goose—a large bird which breeds in the Artic tundra and winters in more southern marshes

Spruce—an evergreen pine tree

Spruce cone—the pinecone from a spruce tree

Star—a shining heavenly body visible in the sky at night. Our sun is a star.

Sturgeon glue—glue made by cooking the heads, bones, and scales of a fish until a gelatin is formed

Trickster—someone who fools others

Turnip—a vegetable with edible leaves and root

Warrior—a person experienced in fighting wars

Water buckets—containers usually made from carved wood, woven plant material, or tightly sealed birchbark

White falcon—a magnificent long-winged bird

Yew—an evergreen tree or bush